Destiny of an Artist

The Artistic Journey of

George Petridis

Special Edition

By Melanie Petridis

And

Dr. Nicholas Orfan

Table of Contents   Page

Dedications

First, I wish to thank God for all the countless blessings He has bestowed upon me. Without Him, life would not have happened.

Second, I wish to dedicate this book to Family, especially my beloved Mother and my Father whom I never got to know, to Friends and to Mentors that helped to shape my destiny as an artist and who never gave up on me even when I had.

A special thanks to the Brothers Pedas, Theodore and James, who gave me the encouragement to tell my story.

And thank you to everyone who will read this book and in a small way help a big cause by supporting the arts and helping the youth of our future.

PROLOGUE

The world was at war. Greece said no to the war and to Benito Mussolini. But Mussolini came anyway and the Greeks defeated him and sent him back to Italy. The Italians, however, had a super weapon in their arsenal. Like a terrible wind in a raging storm, it swept into Greece from the North. The Nazis were here to stay. And the Nazis took food from the people and they were left hungry. They kept the fishermen from going to sea and the people of Greece were starving. It was in this storm of famine and occupation that I, George Petridis, was born. This is my personal testimonial of survival, of life and of discovery. This is about destiny. And so begins that journey in September of 1940.

I was born in the suburb of Athens, Greece to the youngest sister of three. My oldest aunt was married to a Greek American in Pennsylvania. The rest of my relatives including my older brother, Kostas, or Gaston as he prefers to be called, and my younger sister lived in Paleo Falero close to the beach. My mother, Elpiniki, was a widow as my father, whom I barely remember, was killed in the war. My father, Adamantios, was a sea captain in the merchant marines and, as I would someday be told, an artist, too. My father's family hailed from Constantinople, Turkey. Grandfather Petridis was an Orthodox priest married to a very beautiful woman, Grandmother. One night, the Ottoman Turks came and took my grandmother away. The men searched for her but were forced to abandon any hope of finding their beloved wife and mother as the Turks forcibly removed Greeks and Armenians from Turkey. Constantinople became Istanbul. My family fled to Greece where my father came to know my mother. My mother's family also came from the old Byzantine city of Constantinople. They were a successful family of merchants. The Baritou family fled to the Aegean island of Karpathos.

Adamantios was the second captain of his ship. One day the Germans demanded that my father's vessel be used to transport fuel to Istanbul. The First Captain refused to make this run knowing how dangerous it would be. The British had blockaded the waters surrounding Greece in order to prevent the Nazis from sending or receiving supplies. Both American and British aircraft bombed any ship suspected of carrying these supplies no matter what flag the ships sailed under. My father agreed to captain the boat despite my mother's vehement protests. He had been offered good pay to do this and his poor family needed to eat. So Adamantios went to sea. His ship was bombed and all the crew including my father were lost.

My mother, Elpiniki or Niki as she was sometimes called, a Karpathian, was young, petite and very pretty. She was left alone to raise the children and that was no easy task. As the youngest sister of three, she did not inherit anything from the family. Instead my mother was expected to get an education and thus earn her own income. She received a small pension from my father's passing and was a teacher but it was not always enough. And so my brother and I often went out in search of food or the means to earn a little money.

After the Nazis left in 1944, Greece went to war with itself. A civil war that further ravaged the country continued up until 1949. This was the world of my childhood. Life during those years was mostly about survival. Living would come later.

"Destiny"

Author's Note

The prologue is to serve as an introduction to help explain the environment from which the life and destiny of George Petridis was forged. Moreover this is for his children so that they may know their family's history. Too often the past passes away into obscurity. I believe it is important to know where we come from as much as it is to know where we are going. So to my sons and his, I give them this brief prologue in the hope that perhaps one of them will continue telling the story of their ancestors for many years into the future. –Melanie Petridis

George [middle right], Gaston [right], Elpiniki [middle left], Eva [left]

I was twelve when this photo was taken. This was the time of the 'Flower Boy'. My older brother Gaston [Costas] and younger sister Eva along with my dear sweet Mother are standing with me in this photo.

George [top right], Thomas [top left], Gaston [bottom middle], Nicholas [bottom right], Kostas [bottom left]

We were the beach boys at this age. I am around twelve years old here. Thomas was my best friend and accomplice in the 'Flower Boy' exploits. Nicholas, Thomas' older brother, taught us how to fix and sell the flowers.

Chapter One - The Flower Boy

It was late in the summer of 1952. I was a deeply tanned twelve year old with blonde hair bleached by the sun and sea. During the day it was hot and dry. You could smell the pines, the dry grasses and wild sage. Fermenting figs permeated the air with a sweet almost pungent smell. In the coolness of the early morning, my friends and I would go in search of jasmine vines that grew on the walls surrounding homes and villas. We would cut the flowers, tie them in a bundle with pine needles, and place them in a basket in which a soaked cloth had been placed. The basket of bouquets would sit in the shade so as to keep the jasmine fresh and cool.

Come afternoon everything would go quiet except for the buzzing of locusts and chirping of cicadas. This was the time of siesta. It was too hot to do much else. All work stopped until five o'clock in the evening. Sometimes instead of sleeping, I would go down to the sea. The water was cool and refreshing. I loved not only to swim but to dive. Sometimes I would catch fish to eat with a spear while snorkeling. Other times I would go diving and collect shellfish like sea urchins. Some of these I would take to the taverns and sell them for a little money.

When the sun went down the air cooled and life returned to the streets. People went out and activities resumed. Shops reopened for a few hours. As the evening turned to night, the taverns, restaurants, and nightclubs would also open their doors for business. Old men sat in coffee shops playing backgammon and talked of the latest political gossip. Children would go to the parks to play while women visited each other to share the local news and play cards. Young couples would walk along the promenade by the beach. And my friends and I would go out into the night to seek our fortune.

The stars were bright and the air refreshing. The small white jasmine flowers open at night to release their delicate perfume into the evening air. This was the time my friends and I would go out to the different restaurants and clubs to peddle our now fully bloomed jasmine bouquets to patrons. All of the restaurants would let us inside so we could sell our flowers except one, Trocadero, an exclusive, glamorous and expensive nightclub by the sea.

This was fine until the end of summer. By late September, business was slow for the restaurants and night clubs as tourists went home and vacations ended. The only place that remained busy was the one forbidden to us, Trocadero. This exclusive nightclub was almost on the sea itself. It was perched forty feet or so above the water on rocks and stilts. At night you would hear beautiful music coming from inside the walls of the club as the surf lapped at the rocks below. It was an alluring and irresistible temptation to a pair of hungry boys looking to sell some flowers. And perhaps more than just making some money, we wanted to see inside this forbidden place.

So one night when business had slowed in our usual places of work, Thomas, my skinny friend, and I set out for Trocadero. Tom was and always has been very lean. He had a dark complexion, a Roman nose and hair that is jet black to this day. Thomas had three brothers and a sister. It was his older brother, Nick, who showed us how to cut and keep the jasmine until we could set out at night to peddle our wares.

As Thomas and I approached Trocadero, we could hear soft music drifting out into the night air beckoning us to come closer. The place was very busy and we were very hungry. Thomas and I could not go inside so we set up

shop outside to catch customers entering and leaving.

Tom started to complain about his empty belly.

"I'm so hungry and this place is so busy," he whined.

"How are we going to make money if we can't go inside?"

"I'm hungry too," I replied. Thinking of how the noise

from my stomach was becoming louder than the music

coming from inside Trocadero, I formed a plan. A popular

peddler version of Blind Man's Bluff would suffice.

"Thomas, forget the flowers tonight," I said.

Many people knew that after the war, land mines

and live artillery shells were still lying about in the fields

around Athens. Often children running and playing in these

places would come across explosive devices and set one off

with terrible consequences. Many were killed and others

badly maimed and often blinded. I had seen some of those

children myself. So it was my idea for one of us to beg and

the other to play the blind boy. Thomas would do the begging as he could sound more pitiful and I would be the poor sightless child in dire need of a charitable coin or two. We sat near the entrance to Trocadero. It was a dark night and Tom started calling. I made sure to stay in the shadows. All was perfect for staging our little charade.

"Help us please! Could you help my poor blind brother?" Thomas pleaded with great pathos in his voice. He looked more pathetic than me. "My brother lost his eyes to a mine. We have many brothers and sisters to feed. Please help!" Tom's pleading was so desperate that even my eyes started to well up with tears.

We watched as a shiny large car drove up to the entrance where we had stationed ourselves. A well-dressed middle-aged woman stepped out of the limousine. As she walked to the door she couldn't help but hear Thomas' pitiful plead for aid. The lady turned to look at us and stopped to take something from her purse. She came closer to get a better look at me. With her eyes squinting she tried to peer into my face which was cloaked in shadow. "Oh my, this is a terrible thing to happen to such a poor dear boy. You lost your beautiful eyes," she sadly exclaimed. And with that she placed a coin in my outstretched hand.

I slipped the coin into my pocket. The lady then started rummaging through her purse again. "This could be our lucky night!" I thought. She was going to give us more money. Instead of coins, she pulled out a book of matches. "You are such a lovely child," commented the charitable woman. She tried to light a match. "I want to see your face better. It's so dark here."

It suddenly dawned on me what she intended to do with that match. Before she could hold the lighted match to my face, I jumped up from where I was seated and started to run. The very startled lady stood there with her mouth agape but no sound came out. Tom, seeing what had happened, started jumping up and down in a most joyful manner. "It's a miracle! It's a miracle! He saw the light!" he shouted gleefully. "My brother can see!" And with that, Thomas ran off to join me in the night. The miracle for us was that with a single coin, we had full bellies for a week.

The following week our stomachs were groaning again. Food was on our minds. So Tom and I decided to return to Trocadero to tempt our luck once more.

Summer was coming to an end and autumn was fast approaching. The other restaurants and clubs were becoming less busy and so were we. But Trocadero was always packed with people because of the many famous celebrities who entertained there.

Thomas and I were standing in the same spot outside the nightclub for the second time. Tom's stomach was growling somewhat loudly and he started to moan.

"George," he started whining, "I'm so hungry! How are we going to sell our flowers? Everyone is inside and they won't let us go in. Why?" And Tom started to cry.

I too was very hungry. I was also curious to see inside this place forbidden to us. The music floated out beyond the confines of the stone walls into the night air. It was like a siren calling to sailors to come close to the shore only to have their ship crash on the rocks and sink. The popular singer, Fotis Polimeris, had that soft, romantic voice that seemed in tandem rhythm with the sound of the sea. It was a beautiful night with a half moon and a million stars to fill the blackness of the sky. The siren's call overcame me. All resistance was lost as I announced my intentions to my best friend.

I turned to the still moaning, teary-eyed Thomas and proclaimed, "I'm not going to do the blind boy act tonight. Give me your flowers please. I am going to go inside." And with that I took Tom's flower bouquets and put them all into my basket.

A look of alarm appeared on Tom's face. He started pleading with me not to attempt this brazen act. "Don't go George! Please don't do this! What if they catch you? They will surely punish you and it will be very bad."

"Thomas, if I don't do this, then you will stay hungry," I responded. "I'll be just fine. Wait for me." And with that I disappeared into the darkness. I made my way to the back of the club by the beach and rocks. Scrambling over the rocks I reached the wall. It was a short climb from there and finally I was inside. I stood there for a second taking in the view. It was like a great hall in some grand palace. The room was spacious with a marble floor and large columns. It was softly lit creating an atmosphere of romance. Each table was lavishly set with fine china and real silverware. The richness of it all was absolutely mesmerizing for a poor boy like me looking to peddle a few flower bouquets for some money so I could eat. The entire place was filled with wealthy clientele. People were laughing, drinking, dancing, and enjoying their private conversations. Others were leaning back in their chairs with an almost trancelike demeanor taking in the soft voice and moving guitar strumming of Polimeris and his band of musicians. The sea breezes trickled into the club adding to the dreamy atmosphere.

With an air of confidence, I approach the table nearest to me. It was a table full of fancy couples enjoying themselves, laughing and toasting each other with their drinks. I reached into my basket and lifted a bouquet of my best jasmine. I held it out to a young lady so she could digest its sweet perfume. With a sigh and a smile, she delighted in its loveliness. Her husband gave me a coin for the flowers. Soon everyone sitting at the table wanted my jasmine and I had no more bouquets left to sell. Happy with this success I put the money in my pocket. I was grinning from ear to ear and just about to turn around when a big angry looking man, the waiter, came up behind me. Before I had seen him, his big hand gave me a very hard and most painful slap to the side of my head. The force of the blow knocked me down onto the hard marble floor. My empty basket flew across the room. For a moment I was completely disoriented. As I struggle to get up, dizziness and pain overcame me. Stars not seen in the sky whirled around my aching head. Perhaps these were new constellations not yet named. Everyone at the table was watching and a few of them were talking loudly and gesturing somewhat wildly with the waiter. In my anger at having been so cruelly brutalized by this child slapping villain, I looked to throw something at him. With a quick glance I saw a nearby table. No one was seated there. However, it was set with fine porcelain china, silver flatware, and crystal glasses. I reached out and grabbed the edge of the tablecloth. With all my might I pulled it to the floor. Everything on that table crashed loudly to the marble breaking and shattering. The abrupt noise brought silence to Trocadero. The music stopped and no one spoke. Only the ageless sound of the sea could be heard. It felt like a millions eyes were staring at me. Then I saw that angry bull of a waiter coming toward me with raised fists. My eyes opened wide. Frightened for my life, I panicked and looked for a quick exit. The waiter was fast approaching so I took my only option for escape. I had to go out from where I had entered. I jumped up onto the wall. For just a moment I turned my head and looked back. Just as the waiter tried to lay his heavy hands on me, I leaped into the darkness.

It was a forty foot fall into the murky sea below. I could not see where I was going. There were many dangerous rocks in the water surrounding Trocadero and the blackness of the night obscured everything. I was flying blind. My feet hit the water first and to my great relief it was deep. I had avoided striking the rocks directly but only by inches. A burning sensation raked my back as I scraped a rock on entering the crashing surf. The stinging subsided as the cold inky water enveloped my body. I started swimming for the beach. It truly was a miracle that I was not killed. God had helped me to survive.

Meanwhile, Tom heard the commotion coming from inside the club and knew that I had been discovered. He worriedly ran back and forth from one side of the restaurant to the other trying to see something. But it was too dark and the walls built high against the prying eyes of flower boys. Thomas had warned me that something terrible would happen if I got caught? What if his best friend was captured, tortured or even dead? Thomas hoped with all his heart that I had escaped. How would he explain this to my mother? He dreaded the thought. A very frightened Tom raced towards the beach. Perhaps I might be found there. Frantically he started calling, "George! George! Where are you? Oh, please answer! George!" And he started to cry. At first, only the waves crashing on the beach answered his calls mocking his hopes of finding me alive and safe.

Having survived that harrowing dive into the sea, I swam a short distance to the shore. As I pulled myself out of the surf and stumbled onto dry land, I heard a familiar voice calling my name. There was poor Tom standing alone and crying. "Thomas, I'm here!" I said. When Thomas saw me wet and haggard from my near-death ordeal, the look on his face was one of pure shock, almost like he had seen a ghost. "Is that really you, George?" he asked. "Do you know how worried I was about you? Why are you so wet? What happened?" continued Tom with the questions. He was thrilled and relieved to see his friend alive and walking.

We began the long walk home. As I was telling Thomas the story of what took place inside Trocadero, I suddenly remembered the money I had put in my pocket. "Oh, my gosh," I thought to myself. "What if I have lost the money?" All that effort and risk would have been for nothing. I felt inside my wet pockets. To my relief it was all there. Another miracle! I smiled and told Tom that we would eat very well all week.

We went straight to my house. It was late and my mother had gone to bed. At least that is what I hoped. Tom and I quietly went inside. The money was still very wet so we carefully laid it out to dry. Proud of my accomplishment, I had forgotten that my back was cut and bruised by the rough sandpaper surface of the rocks when I leaped into the sea. A gasp startled the two of us. I turned around to see my mother standing in the doorway. Apparently she was up and very much awake. My mother started to cry and rushed over to me. She grabbed me and frantically pulled off my still damp shirt. To my horror, I saw why she was upset. The back of my once white shirt was stained crimson with blood. My back was bruised and cut. Rock rash had left the skin raw and tender.

"Oh my dear son, how did this happen to you? Where have you been?" she cried. "What have you done this time?" My mother was most anxious and on the verge of hysteria. Then she saw the money laid out on the table behind Tom and me. She paused and her face changed "And where did you get that?"

I confessed everything to her as she found some alcohol. My mother worried about infection and poured the alcohol onto the wounds on my back. I was disinfected. It was only at that moment that I fully realized how many open sores and cuts I had received from those rocks. I winced. The alcohol made my injuries feel worse. At least my mother felt better.

But my mother like all mothers continued to chide me about how stressed I had made her. "You could have been killed!" she scolded. "What would I do if you were badly hurt or even killed? You have to think before you go leaping into the unknown! It really is a miracle that you are alive." When she turned her head I could see a tiny smile on her face despite the tears in her eyes.

The next morning I woke to hear a familiar voice calling me. "George! George!" It was Nick, Tom's older brother, walking up to the door with a newspaper in his hand.

I answered the door and let him inside. "George, where were you and my brother last night? Did the two of you go to Trocadero?" Nick inquired. His eyes were somewhat stern and he seemed at that moment a little older than his age.

"Yes, we were there. Why do you ask?" I replied matter of factly.

"Here, look at this," he said. Nick made me take the newspaper. "Look at this!" He pointed to the article. "They say you are dead!"

"Trocadero"

I took the paper and my eyes opened wide. I could not believe what I saw. There in bold black ink was the headline, "Ten Year Old Boy Killed at Trocadero!" The article went on to describe how a waiter from Trocadero drove a young flower boy to his death. The waiter had chased the boy over the wall, down onto the rocks and into the sea below. Authorities searched but could find no body. It was believed that the boy had either drowned or died instantly on the rocks and that the body had been taken out to sea by an undertow from a strong current. The poor flower boy was gone forever but would haunt the memory of those who had been present that fateful night at Trocadero.

George and Cousin Vana

I was nineteen in this photo. I had recently

graduated from high school and was about to embark on a

journey that would lead me to my destiny as an artist.

Chapter Two – Finding Destiny

Years passed by and finally I was a young man ready to embark on adventures far from home. I had worked at odd jobs throughout my teenage years from selling the fish I caught to learning the trade of laying mosaic floors. But now having graduated from high school, I had to decide my future. In order to find work and to attend a university, I would have to leave Greece. At that time young Greeks had three options. We could go to Australia, Canada or Germany. My older brother, Gaston, had already left for Canada. I, however, wanted to be closer to home so I could more easily return to Greece and help take care of my mother. I chose to go to Germany where I would work and attend a university. And so I packed my bags and headed off to the future.

Travel options were somewhat limited in those

years. People went by boat or train and not by plane. First, I took a ferry to Italy and then from there I traveled by railcar through the towns and countryside of Italy and Switzerland to my final destination, Dusseldorf, West Germany. When returning to Greece, I had to take a train through Austria and Yugoslavia. Either way, it was always a scenic route and gave me the opportunity to see the beauty of the European landscape.

One might wonder how and why a Greek boy like me could afford to go to Germany to study and work. After World War II, Germany agreed to pay war reparations to help rebuild those nations they had occupied and ravaged. My mother had received some of that money which helped her to buy the land on which we lived. The money also assisted young adults like me to go to Germany and study at their universities. I took advantage of this opportunity and went to a new country with the hope of studying medicine and becoming a doctor someday.

Having arrived in the beautiful but rainy city of Dusseldorf, I finally settled in and started my studies at Heinrich Heine University while taking a job in a local factory that manufactured guitar strings. It took me a year and a half to learn to read and speak German. You had to learn German first before you could begin to study medicine.

One sunny and cheerful morning while on my way to work, I passed a newsstand on the street. I stopped briefly to buy a newspaper when a magazine caught my interest. I skimmed through the magazine and saw an article about a princess and a Greek. I bought the magazine and took it with me to work. During a coffee break, I finished reading the story about the princess. It was about Princess Beatrix of the Netherlands. She was only a year older than me and not bad looking. Princess Beatrix was also extremely wealthy and she was looking to meet a Greek man! Imagine that! A Greek man, I thought to myself." Hmmm, I am Greek, about her age, and good looking! And I am only two hours away by train. This could be an opportunity." I was excited to think that this could be a dream come true. Besides, I needed a break from my work and studies and this would make for a pleasant diversion and an interesting new adventure.

So I made up my mind to meet the princess and make her dream come true. I purchased a train ticket and was soon on my way to The Hague, Seat of the Royal Court of the Netherlands. It was late afternoon by the time I arrived at my destination. Because it was late I went to find a hotel. Fortunately, there was one with a vacancy not far from the City Center and I reserved a room for the night. Now that I had a place to sleep there was enough time to go out and explore the city. I felt very happy to be there and was glad to have the opportunity to feel and absorb the atmosphere of a new place.

It was early evening. The sun peeked through the clouds foretelling the lovely sunset to come. I started exploring the maze of streets lined with long rows of houses interspersed with canals and arched bridges. After a time, I began to notice that all the houses looked similar to each other.

All of this seemed so very different from Greece and even from Germany where the houses are more varied in color, shape and size. It was nevertheless beautiful and I was enjoying the moment completely. Before I knew it, time had passed and it was getting dark. The weather changed too and a gorgeous sunset was not to be. The clouds overtook what was left of a setting sun and soon it started to drizzle. The bright cheery day turned to a dull misty gray twilight. Suddenly it dawned on me that I was very lost. Concern turned to worry. To make matters worse, I had forgotten the name of my hotel. Anxiety was overwhelming me. I was in a new place among strangers..

What was I to do? How was I going to find help when I did not speak the language?

The only thing I thought to do was to approach different people and ask in German if someone could help me to find my way. Suddenly a tall hooded figure appeared out of the rainy fog and stood before me like some Dutch ghost from a time long gone. Nervously I inquired if this phantom spoke German. "Sprechen Sie Deutch?"

"Ja," answered the specter in a deep voice which surprised me. It was difficult to see his face.

I was relieved however to finally find someone who might be able to render aid to a lost soul. "Please sir can you help me to find my hotel?" I quickly asked this apparition standing before me. I was afraid that he would suddenly vanish like some wispy spirit. "It seems I have lost my way in all this rain."

He motioned for me to follow him and proceeded to lead me through the darkness down some narrow alley to his flat. The inside of his small apartment turned out to be a rather bright, cheerful and very neat place. He removed his wet outer wraps and offered to make me hot tea. I gratefully drank this. It helped to take away the chill I was feeling. He then introduced himself as Herr Hans. I was pleased to make his acquaintance and gave him my name. He went into the bedroom and, to my surprise, returned dressed as a woman. He had a wig, red lipstick, a dress and high heels. He poured us both a brandy and said, "don't worry, we'll find your room." Thinking quickly, I told him that I had an adult communicable disease and that I was not allowed to drink alcohol and must return to my hotel right away to take my pills. Hans telephoned the police. With my name they were able to locate the hotel where I was registered. Elated to have the name of the hotel, I thanked Hans and got up to leave. But Hans stopped me. "How long will you be in town?" he asked. "Two weeks," I lied. "I'll call on you in a week when you're feeling better," he said, and stuffed some money in my pocket. He called for a taxi and I soon found myself safe in my hotel room. I packed my things and moved to a hotel blocks away. The kindness afforded me by the Dutch people was memorable.

"Den Hague"

A good night's rest restored both my energy and confidence. The next morning I awoke to sunshine.

Refreshed, I set out in search of a palace and a princess. The Hague City Centre was a large and spacious plaza with many shops, cafes and restaurants. Because many people gathered here and it was very busy, I thought I would find someone who could speak German and, thus, could kindly send me in the direction of Her Royal Highness. As I was searching for someone to guide me, I accidently bumped into a lovely young lady. If I didn't know better, I would have thought that she was the Princess herself. I kindly excused myself and asked if she knew any German. To my delight she did. So I inquired if she knew the way to the palace. "You see I'm Greek and I am looking to meet with Princess Beatrix."

"Why?" she asked with a look of curious puzzlement on her face. "How do you know her?"

"Why? Haven't you heard? I read an article in a magazine describing how the Princess wants to meet a

Greek man and here I am! And who knows, I might be your Prince someday!" I exclaimed.

Finding this all too amusing, the sweet young woman started to laugh. "Oh that's a good one," the girl giggled. She thought I was using this as a pickup line. But on closer inspection she realized that I truly believed the story in the magazine.

I was beginning to wonder if this dream of meeting a fairytale princess was only the stuff of tabloids. Or perhaps I hadn't translated the article well. Either way, I decided rather quickly on a new course of action. After all there was a truly noble woman in front of me and I did not have to search for a well-guarded castle. So I asked the girl if she would like to go somewhere for a coffee. To my delight she accepted my offer. We found a nearby café where the two of us could enjoy each other's company.

First introductions were made. Her name was Heidi and she was half German and half Dutch. That is why Heidi knew how to speak German. Sipping coffee can be such an ice breaker. She warmed up to me and continued to talk and talk. I found her to be interesting with a great sense of humor. She seemed to like me as well. We chatted away the afternoon. Heidi told me how it was her dream to go to Greece someday. She had heard of its timeless beauty and wonderful climate. Northern Europe did have too many cloudy days as I had come to know, whereas Greece was almost always delightfully sunny. Cloudy, wet weather was a "phenomenon" to Greeks.

Eventually our conversation turned to the object of my visit to the Netherlands, Her Royal Highness, Princess Beatrix. "Really, why would you want to meet her, George? I heard she has a glass eye!" Heidi kindly informed me.

"I didn't know that," I said thanking her for the warning. With all due respect, I really did not want to meet a one-eyed princess. And we both had a good laugh.

As it was late in the day, Heidi proposed that we meet her father and then perhaps get something to eat. I agreed and followed her across the plaza to a side street not far from the hotel where I was lodging. Instead of taking me to her house, Heidi led me to her father's place of work, his art studio. Little did I know that this would be the beginning of a great journey that would become my destiny. As I entered the room, something came over me. It was the first time I had ever been in a working studio. My eyes opened wide as I took in the beauty of all the colorful works of art. The paintings excited a creative urge within me and I felt compelled to learn how to do this. I needed to do this. Heidi introduced me to an older gentleman whose clothes were splattered with splotches of color from paint that had escaped its intended mark. His name was Herr

Johannes and he was an artist. With great elation I shook his painted hand feeling the electricity of the moment. I had just met someone of great importance. He gladly took us on a walking tour of his studio, carefully introducing me to each of his oil paintings. They were as much his children as was Heidi. The more I saw the more I felt the need to know the secrets of putting yourself on a piece of canvas. Your emotions would become colors and brushstrokes and your thoughts would be visually displayed for all to see. Yes! I had to know how to do this. So finally I gathered the courage and asked Herr Johannes if he would please be my teacher.

To my amazement, he agreed. He seemed pleased to be able to pass his wealth of artistic knowledge on to another generation and offered his gracious gift of mentoring. However, the master had conditions which I readily accepted. This was the opportunity of a lifetime and little did I know how much it would forever change the direction of my life. His terms were rather simple. I had only to agree to travel to The Hague every weekend from Germany for Master Johannes' private art lessons. So I began the weekly two hour trek from Dusseldorf to the art studio in The Hague where I apprenticed myself to a master of Dutch impressionism. I wanted to find my innermost artistic self.

Eight months passed quickly. I had a deep ocean of knowledge to explore. Painting is part learned technique, part practiced self-expression. It is the applied knowledge of how to mix and choose your colors and how to understand the nature of form and light. But the rest is up to you because it is your vision. As my talent in art was developing, my feelings for the Master's daughter were also growing. Heidi was just as enamored of me. One day with her parents' blessing, I proposed to her. We were happily engaged.

Now, I had a new future to think about and someone to share it with. So one day after considerable thought, I approached Johannes about my plans. My decision was to quit painting and concentrate more on my medical studies. The hope was to become a medical doctor and to earn enough money to support a family. As far as I was concerned there was no money to be had in art and I wanted to give Heidi a good life. Needless to say, Master Johannes was not very pleased by this revelation.

"Oh no, George!" exclaimed a shaken Johannes. "This can't be so. You must not quit now! You are too talented George. This is a natural gift from God. I had to have many years of formal training and more years of practice to become what I am today. But you, my dear George, paint so easily. It is a part of you that you were born to express. Please, before you give up your art, promise me one thing. Take your best work and go to Paris. I want you to try to sell something at Montmartre. Only when you have done this and returned here to me will I accept your decision to abandon art."

Because of my deep respect for my mentor and my love for his daughter, I agreed to Johannes' challenge. I left for another country and a new city.

Paris, the City of Lights, was painted gray with rain. It was just my luck to arrive in a new place and be greeted by a shower on the first day. I quickly found a place to stay. Because the evening was still young I decided to go out and experience some of Paris' many wonderful sights. It was still raining and so I found dry refuge at a café on the grandest Parisian street, the Champs-Elysees. Darkness had settled in and Paris' famous nightlife emerged. Street lights cast their warm glow onto the wet pavement where it shimmered and reflected like sunlight dancing on the surface of a river. Cafes and restaurants filled with couples while music drifted out into the evening air. People bustled about hiding from the drizzle underneath brightly colored umbrellas. The ambiance of this romantic scene unfolding before me caused a spark of inspiration for a new painting, "Paris in the Rain." I would come to paint this scene many times. Rain helped to create a nostalgic moment that I would continue to use in a beautiful way.

The next morning I awoke to sunshine. I was now eager to go find that place Master Johannes had told me about, Montmartre. I was going to display my paintings there. Montmartre is best known for its white church, Sacré-Cœur, the Basilica of the Sacred Heart. But Montmartre is also known as the Village of Artisans. Many famous artists like Monet, Picasso, Dali, and van Gogh had their studios in this district. And now I would have the distinction and honor of being in a place revered by fellow artists and lovers of beauty. I went to the Place du Tertre and found many artists painting and selling their art. This was the place Johannes spoke of. It looked very promising and so I set up my things and readied myself for business. I carefully displayed several small paintings hoping they would be acceptable to the discriminating tastes of French art lovers. It wasn't long before a young couple walking hand-in-hand stroll by my display. To my surprise they stop to look at my paintings. They pointed to three of my art pieces and then gestured toward me. They wanted to buy all three. I knew only a little French but did my best to tell them how much and give them a fair price. The man took out his leather billfold and handed me the money. It was more than I had asked. The two people smiled and departed happily clutching their new masterpieces. I was elated. I couldn't believe that I had just sold my first three paintings and so quickly too. I had not been there for more than an hour. Truly, God was trying to tell me something and Herr Johannes must have been His Angel sent to keep me on the path to my destiny. Maybe I truly was meant to be an artist. The experience of knowing that people actually loved my work had me jumping and dancing for joy. Zorba the Greek could not have danced better. Unfortunately that happiness was short lived. The other artists were complaining that I had no permit and called the police. A pair of uniformed officers approached me and inquired as to whether I had a permit to display my work. I tried to explain in broken French that I did not have a permit because no one told me that I needed one.

"Oui, monsieur, you must have one for this area. You can't display here! There is another place further down from here for artists like you," said the policeman gruffly. "Since this is your first time we can let you go but only if you give us the money you made here."

"What happens if I keep the money?" I asked these fine officers of the law. I had just experienced a moment of great happiness and now this? They wanted me to give them the first dollar I ever earned through art and just walk away? That first sale was my moment of truth. That was the sale that sealed my destiny as an artist. I couldn't possibly give them that money because of what it represented to me.

"You will go to jail if you don't give us the money," replied the policeman. "Surely you don't want to spend the night in a cell?"

"Oh but I do!" I retorted back to the officer curtly. "I am keeping my money!" I was not giving up my first sale. One night behind bars was a small penalty to pay for having made some people very happy and the world a more beautiful place. And so I was hauled off to prison as a criminal of the arts.

That night I cozied up in a jail cell with a new found friend. He was an Italian artist who had made the same mistake as me. I spoke better Italian than French so we were able to converse with each other throughout the night. He started to tell me about his experience in the Place du

Tertre. He did not know that you needed a special permit to exhibit and sell art there. The police came and gave him a choice and so he chose French hospitality and his hard earned money. We could not go to sleep so conversation kept us company. His name was Roberto and he was an artist of gab. He continued on into the morning chatting away about his future plans. When he was released from prison, Roberto planned to travel to Toronto, Canada. He heard that business in Canada was good and hassle free.

"In Canada, I will be able to be the artist I was meant to be," declared Roberto with proud self-assurance. "Perhaps you can come to Canada someday too. We could meet in Toronto."

The next morning we found ourselves free men. Roberto and I parted company having enjoyed our stay at one of Paris' finest lodgings. Perhaps sometime in the future I would see Roberto again. Destiny would write the chapters of my life without free previews.

I returned to The Hague a new man. Herr Johannes was eager to hear about my French excursion and how well I had fared. "Do I still want to quit painting?" he asked. Johannes was elated when I told him how Paris had taught me to love and protect the artist within. There would be no more thoughts of medical school. I presented him with my new painting, "Paris in the Rain." He was stunned.

"Paris in the Rain"

"This is wonderful George," he exclaimed with exuberance. "The painting is absolutely stunning!" The wise old Master could see the artist I was becoming. He was happy to know his apprentice had not forsaken the artist's life.

One day not long after my return to The Hague, I decided to call my brother, Gaston, who was now living in Canada. We spoke to each other for a long time. I told him about my engagement to Heidi and my new career. Gaston told me that I should come to Toronto to see him. He was missing his brother and family. I missed him too but would have to think about his invitation. But Gaston was persuasive. He would even make the arrangements necessary to travel. I would not have to worry about a thing. I became excited remembering where Roberto, my ex-con artist friend, was going to find success as an artist. The Americas held more promise than Europe for a young artist seeking to earn a living from his calling.

The decision was made. Gaston would not take no for an answer. But I had to explain my plans to Heidi and her father. I told them that I had been invited by my brother to Toronto and that he was already making arrangements. I explained that after seeing Gaston and assessing the chances of having a successful art career in Canada, I would come back to marry Heidi. Perhaps we would go together to live in Toronto, I promised. Heidi sadly agreed that I should go. Canada was a new and unexplored opportunity.

I left The Hague and went back to Dusseldorf to make preparations for overseas travel. The factory where I worked had to be given notice that I was quitting and issue my final paycheck. Also the university had to be informed of my desire to leave. I had fallen in love with a beautiful girl and with beauty itself. I had tasted success and dreamed of adventure. I was no longer George the medical student, I was George the artist.

I had finished packing my few belongings when I received a phone call from Master Johannes. He was distraught and with great difficulty broke the tragic news to me. There had been a terrible accident. A drunken truck driver had driven his vehicle into a crowded market. Heidi and several others were killed. I could not believe what I was hearing. This had to be a nightmare. How could this be true? I quickly returned to The Hague. The family and I were devastated by this terrible tragedy. I waited for the sun to come out.

My brother called again. "George, you must come to Canada," he said. "All the arrangements are made. It will do you good."

I promised my dear Master Johannes and his wife that I would keep in touch. He had forever changed my life and his daughter would always live in my heart. I would miss them and the life we shared in The Hague. I departed for a new world across a wide sea.

CN Tower in Toronto

Chapter Three – New World

Upon arriving in Toronto, I saw my brother Gaston

for the first time in several years. As we left the airport, I could not help but notice that it wasn't raining. Perhaps this was a sign of better things to come. We spent the first few hours of our reunion talking about all that had happened to us in the last couple of years. He was working as a mechanic and making good money. I proudly told him of my new found vocation as an artist. He just looked at me and said nothing. I continued by offering to teach him how to paint. I told Gaston about Paris and how I was now an ex-con. "Art has its painful moments but still can be profitable in the end," I said.

"I will make you an artist dear brother. This way you can make your own money because you will be your own boss," I declared.

"Are you crazy George?" returned Gaston. "I will starve!"

"Not if you're good," I replied. "And I know you will be the best!"

Later that day, we called our mother to tell her that her much-loved sons were safely reunited in Canada. I took the phone and told her enthusiastically how promising everything looked for a young artist seeking opportunity here. Then I announced how she was going to have not one but two artist sons and that Gaston had agreed to be my first student. For a moment the phone went silent.

"Oh my goodness!" exclaimed our mother. "Did I ever tell you that your father was an artist too?" This surprised both of us. We never knew.

It was now clear to me why I had a natural gift for art. My brother, in time, would become a very successful artist as well. Gaston and I had inherited this natural ability. I asked my mother why it took her twenty-three years to tell us about our dad.

"You know, my son, how difficult it was for me to raise all of you children during the war after your father was killed. I just didn't think about it until now," she explained with some sadness in her voice. My mother sacrificed so much for us. But I was very glad to have this revelation about my father. My rebirth as an artist was no accident.

Over the next few days Gaston took me to see the sights of Toronto. Everything here was new. In Europe, many buildings are old and even ancient. Many homes in Europe have stood for multiple centuries. In comparison, even the oldest homes here in Canada seem like infants. Toronto was a busy city, very clean and modern. Moreover, there was plenty of green space. You had to drive a long way to go from place to place.

Gaston surprised me by taking me to Danforth Avenue, Toronto's Greek town. Here there were Greek shops, restaurants, and clubs. To me it was like a touch of home. We parked the car and I got out. While walking around and taking in the nostalgic atmosphere of Danforth, I was amazed to bump into people I knew from Greece. Wow! They too had come to Canada in order to find success and the "good life". With so many friends here, I knew this was the place for me. I felt confident and happy with my decision to leave Europe. Greek town became a surrogate home for me and I visited often.

One sultry summer evening while wandering about Danforth Avenue looking for familiar souls, a restaurant billboard caught my attention. The place was called Neraida and it featured live music. But it was the name of the performer that made me pause in surprise. There flashing in brilliant lights on the sign above the club was the name of Fotis Polimeris! I had to go inside.

As I was waiting to be seated I noticed someone very familiar. Aleko, it seemed, was the local photographer who would snap pictures of people sitting at their tables while being entertained by Greek singers or musicians. He was my good friend from Athens. We knew each other from our days on the beach under a warm Greek sun. Now he and his Spartan wife, Aleka were living in Toronto and were seated at a nearby table. They graciously invited me to sit with them. I wondered if all of this was fate or mere coincidence. This was indeed becoming a very memorable night.

"Aleko, my friend, how good to see you. What a small world it is!" I exclaimed. "Aleko, would you do a small favor for me? Would you ask the singer to come to our table during his break?"

Aleko gladly obliged leaving his wife and me to enjoy the sentimental music and our delicious Greek meal while he made his rounds. The music reminded me of my boyhood along the shore of the Mediterranean Sea and of a particular evening when a young street urchin dove off a cliff to escape an angry waiter. Finally Mr. Polimeris came over to our table and politely greeted us. "Did you call for me?" he inquired. "Is there something I can do for you?" He looked around at each of us smiling.

I smiled back and introduced myself. "Yes," I told him. There was something important I needed to ask him. "Do you remember Trocadero along the beach in Athens some years ago?"

Fotis nodded. "Oh yes I do. It was such a beautiful and glamorous place. I worked that nightclub for many years. It closed about two years ago and the place was torn down. It is a marina now. What a shame to see it go. Trocadero was truly fabulous. So why do you ask? Did you perhaps work there at one time?"

"That is too bad about the place being gone," I said sympathetically. "Do you remember the story about a flower boy who was killed there?"

"Oh gosh, yes!" exclaimed Polimeris taking a step back and shaking his head. "What a tragedy! That poor boy! I remember very well because I was there that terrible night. I have thought about that night too many times." Then Fotis started to tell the story of the flower boy as he had witnessed it many years ago. It was almost a confession through which he was seeking absolution from a nightmare of a memory. "This young boy, maybe ten years old, found his way into Trocadero by coming over a wall in the back. You know they wouldn't allow any peddlers into that place. Too exclusive I guess. Anyway, I was surprised to see someone so young daring enough to come into the club to peddle. That took a lot of guts. I watched him sell flowers at a big table. I was going to stop playing my music and go congratulate this lad for having done what no one

66

else had been able to do when this bloody waiter came up and slapped the boy hard on the head. I think everyone saw the poor kid fall down. The child must have been hurting really badly. Next thing we knew, the boy had pushed over a table and broken everything. I saw the waiter chase the kid and the desperate child jumped the wall and fell to his death. They never did find the body. There was some justice because that nasty waiter went to jail for causing a ten-year-old's death. I will never forget that night," laments Polimeris. "Why do you ask me to remember this horrible tragedy?"

Mr. Polimeris had finished his story. There were tears in my eyes as I too recalled in my mind the details of that fateful evening of my boyhood so long ago. "Mr. Polimeris, you can rest easy," I replied. "The boy is not dead because I am alive! I am the flower boy. You see, I knew how to swim and dive and by God's good grace, I only suffered a few cuts and bruises from the rocks."

Fotis Polimeris paled. His eyes opened wide and his mouth dropped. He put his hand to his head and I thought he was going to faint. "Oh my, are you really him? How can that be? Oh wow!" he exclaimed hoarsely. He was utterly stunned by this revelation.

Smiling, I told him that the man before him was indeed the grown up boy from Trocadero. A still shaken Fotis sat down with us at the table and I continued telling him how I survived the jump and swam to safety.

Polimeris got up and excused himself as his break was over. We shook hands warmly and then he gave me an emotional hug. "You know, I carried that horrible memory with me all my life. Thank you for relieving my mind of that terrible tragedy. I am so thankful you are alive and well." He thanked me again and, during his breaks, Fotis kept coming back to our table where we would reminisce about the past. It was strange how, after many years and many countries, time could circle back upon itself. Who would have guessed that something that happened when I was only a child in Greece would find closure on a different continent thousands of miles away across an ocean?

Canada was a happy place for me. Things looked promising except that my English still needed help. Gaston suggested I look for an English language school. I was eager to start business as an artist but was inhibited by the communication barrier. I needed to be able to converse with the people here.

One day, I was waiting at the bus stop next to my brother's apartment when a car pulled up and two men stopped to ask for directions to downtown Toronto. Their English was accented with what sounded like Greek. "Are you Greek?" I questioned the two of them. And to my delight they said yes.

We started conversing with each other in our native tongue. Introductions were made. Their names were John and Nicholas and it was the latter who did most of the talking. Meanwhile, I missed my bus. In fact, I didn't even notice it stopping. Nick, the conversationalist, went on to tell me that he was from Athens. He identified himself as salesman of sorts and said that John was a friend he had met along the way. I eagerly told them how I too was from Athens and that I was a professional artist! However, my English was poor and I needed to find a school so I could learn the language. John spoke up and told me that there was a school not far from the bus stop. He knew about the school because he had gone there himself. Nicholas was interested in seeing my work as he might be able to help sell my paintings. This meeting would turn out to be providential. Destiny was at work again. All I needed was a ride and Nick and John gladly obliged. They went downtown and I went to school.

After a time, I became very good friends with Nicholas. Eventually Nick, Gaston, and I found work with the Canadian National Railway (CNR). We were given positions as waiters in the passenger cars. For me, this provided good interaction with the public and a chance to practice my English.

One busy morning while serving breakfast aboard the train, I discovered a new word for eggs. The menu offered "eggs done your way". The usual order was for "sunny side up" eggs or as I called them, "sunshine" eggs. But one of the passengers just had to be different. He ordered 'scrambled' eggs. My dark eyebrows went up and I looked at him puzzled. "Come again sir?" I replied.

He looked at me almost indignant. "Scrambled eggs please!" he replied again with some agitation. Maybe this surly passenger thought I was deaf because he spoke more loudly than before.

"I am sorry sir but I don't think we serve that sort of egg," I responded as politely as possible. I was very certain that this egg the customer spoke of was an egg anomaly rarely seen and in my experience never before requested.

"Surely you do," said the hungry man. He was trying his best to stay calm.

"Sorry sir but my English is not so good," I replied sounding as apologetic as possible. "What is 'scrambled'? I don't understand this kind of egg."

The famished man looked at me in a most peculiar manner and then told me to go find the chef. Anxious to get out of this perplexing dilemma I quickly complied. To my relief the cook was Greek. I hurriedly told him there was a problem with one of the customers. This particular patron wanted his eggs 'scrambled'? I had never heard of such a thing.

The chef started to laugh. "Here let me show you! See these eggs?" And he cracked a few into a bowl. "Now you beat the heck out them!" The cook then took a whisk and proceeded to beat the eggs into a frothy liquid of blended white and yellow. He poured the beaten mix into a skillet and fried them up. "Voila 'scrambled' eggs! Now take the order." He handed me the dish.

I quickly returned to the table with the prized plate of hot 'scrambled' eggs. The starving patron was all too happy to finally have his breakfast done his way. I kindly thanked him for his patience with me. The man left me a generous tip despite everything and I was cheerful the rest of the day. My time on the train not only improved my English vocabulary but helped me learn how to deal with many types of people as well. I learned that your customer is always right and a satisfied customer makes for a very good day. My waiter stint would also, uncannily, lead me to my destiny as a self- sufficient artist.

Weeks passed and one day Nicholas and I got a call from the railway. The company wanted us to serve as private waiters for a group of important passengers. They were government ministers and officials who reserved the train for a fishing trip to North Bay. Nick, who always had a nose for a good business opportunity, told me to bring along a couple of my small paintings just in case. So I did and I put them in the back of the dining car where they could be easily seen. I was busy working when one of the other waiters told me that someone in the rear wanted to see me. I turned and went to see who had asked for me and why. Seated in a booth was a middle-aged man who introduced himself as a high level CNR administrator. He then pointed to two of the paintings I had brought aboard.

"Was I in trouble for having done this?" I wondered out loud.

"Oh no," said the official. "Are you the artist? What is your name?"

Relieved that I was not about to be fired, I eagerly responded, "Yes sir! I am the artist. My name is George.

"Well young man, I want to buy these," he said. I was surprised by his proclamation. This was totally unexpected. The officer saw the look of astonishment on my face. "Don't be so surprised. These are really good. I like them and I want to buy them. Why are you working here as a waiter? Don't you know that you should be painting and selling your work? You have talent my boy!" With that he gave me his hand.

"Canadian Wilderness"

I was flabbergasted. This important man really liked my paintings. I told him that I was new in this country and I was looking to become a professional artist someday. However I didn't know where to display my art.

He thought for a moment. "George, I am really good at judging people's character. I can see you have a good personality and are sincere about your painting. Besides, I love good art, especially something new and fresh. You have all of this. I think I can help you."

To my delight, he did indeed help me to find a place where I could stay and devote more of my time to creating new works of art. Thank goodness I had listened to Nicholas when he told me to bring those paintings to work that day. Destiny has a strange way of working. If there is one thing that I learned from this experience, it was to seize the moment and not pass up what might be a golden opportunity. Now, with Nick's gift of salesmanship, I was beginning to earn a living as an artist.

Nicholas was tall for a Greek, fair complexioned, and blue-eyed. Good natured and light hearted. Doing business with Nick was always a pleasure. However, he did have one unusual habit. He was a night owl. Nicholas would venture out into the evening in order to sell my art outside of restaurants and other public places. On one such evening, he had great success with a particular painting of mine. This art piece depicted the Toronto skyline and its most iconic architectural element, the famous Canadian National Tower, reflected in the cold waters of Lake Erie. The tower was one of the highest free-standing structures in the world. I had never seen a building so tall. It was popular with tourists, locals, and me. I loved its revolving tower restaurant and lookout platforms where the views were just breathtaking. I simply had to paint this tower. Fortunately, the painting was very popular with art patrons. Nick managed to sell the exact same painting ten times. He delayed delivery by saying that the painting still needed some finishing work and that he would send the piece once it was complete and the oil had dried.

I was sound asleep when someone shook me to consciousness. Startled, I awoke suddenly to find Nicholas hovering over my bed. When my eyes adjusted and I could see it was only Nick and not some night marauder, I gruffly replied "Nick? What's going on? It's the middle of the night!"

Nicholas turned on the light, half blinding my still sleepy eyes. "George, you have to get up! You have to start painting," he exclaimed. "Here! I will make you coffee."

"What? Why now at this hour? Do you know what time it is?" I grumpily asked Nick. I was not a night owl like him. I also enjoyed sleeping on a normal schedule.

"George! I just sold your painting of the tower to ten different customers. They are waiting for you to finish it. It is a very popular piece you know." Nick explained his dilemma. His impossible promises were now mine to keep.

"What? I can't make ten paintings exactly the same! How am I going to do that?" This was definitely a problem and my foggy, sleep deprived brain still was trying to grasp the enormity of what Nick was requesting. Now I had ten problems to solve.

"You don't have too," said Nick. "Just make them similar. Besides it was dark when they saw the painting." He smiled at me and it was then that I understood his genius.

So I jumped out of bed, drank a gallon of coffee, went to my paint box, and got busy mass producing ten paintings of that all too famous Canadian National Tower. It was moments like this that relied upon and sometimes depleted the vigor of my youth.

Nick was a very persuasive and an excellent salesman. He made it possible for me to become a career artist in a new country. Nicholas left Canada and crossed the border into a place known for making dreams come true. The land of endless opportunity awaited us with open arms. At least that is what immigrants, such as us, were led to believe. The United States was the ultimate goal that fueled our imagination. And New York City would be the launching point for this new journey into destiny. Someone told us that if you can make it in New York then you can make it anywhere. I later learned 'someone' was a famous song but the words still rang true.

At first, Nicholas plied his skills in New York while I remained in Toronto. Nick was selling paintings. My art had found a place in the great city of New York. The only problem was that Nick had to constantly commute back and forth to Toronto to get new paintings. Other times, I would find a way to ship him the art. This continued for about a year until he became tired of all the traveling. "George," he implored. "You must come to New York. It is clear that you can work here as an artist and make a good living.

George, please come to the 'Big Apple'!"

Nicholas had kept me so busy painting that I finally gave notice to my employer, the Canadian National Railway, and said my grateful goodbye to Toronto. My dream of being a self-employed professional artist was finally coming true. I could now chart my own course. So I left Canada to begin a new life in America.

"New York City – Manhattan"

Chapter Four – Life in the Apple

New York City was unlike any place I had known. I had lived in many large cities, so why was I awestruck by New York? First, it was beyond big. New York City wasn't just large in area but also in altitude. The buildings were massive and tall. The New York City skyline pierced the clouds. The city was always busy. The kinetic energy there seemed perpetual. Traffic on the streets was constant. The sidewalks and shops were filled with people hustling and bustling about. Day and night there was no rest, no sleep, just constant continuous movement of humans and machines in a landscape of concrete mountains. This titan of cities would be my new home for several years to come. I could see why Nicholas was always occupied. How could you not be with so much happening around you? I could not wait to find Nick and explore this new urban world. Welcome to New York!

As I mentioned, Nick was a guru of marketing. The city that never slept was perfect for a night person like Nick. I couldn't help but think of those long nights with him back in Toronto. He was absolutely elated to see me. Nick was eager to take me around to see the sights and to introduce me to his favorite business districts. One of those areas was 53rd Street. "George, my boy, this is your spot tomorrow," Nick announced happily to me. "You will set up here and paint. Now let's go see the rest of New York!"

So the next morning with the sun beaming brightly I set off to display my work on 53rd Street as Nicholas had instructed. I was located outside a theatre between the Hilton and Americana Hotels. I was ecstatic because it wasn't too long before I started making sales. Nick had left me alone there while he went to display more of my art on another street. People seemed to come from nowhere yet were everywhere. There was always someone ready to buy my work. New York was banishing any blues!

I had been busy since morning on 53rd Street. The day was looking brighter every moment and, before I knew it, several very productive hours had passed. It was only midday and I was eager to see how the rest of the afternoon would go when Nicholas suddenly showed up and surprised me. I cheerfully told him of my great success there.

Before I could speak another word, Nick interrupted and hastily ordered me to pick up everything. "Ok George, that's good but we must go now!" And he started putting my display in our little van.

I helped him with the paintings. "Why do we have to go? I'm doing well here. This is a good place and it is only noon." I was puzzled by his haste to leave.

"We have to hurry because we have only a few hours left to sell in a more exclusive place." Nick quickly explained. "Now let's go!

So with everything packed up, we drove to Fifth Avenue. Immediately I could see that this was a very expensive street. Nick and I were now in Midtown Manhattan. Prestigious shops lined this thoroughfare of the wealthy. It was in front of one of these stores that Nicholas told me to park the van. However I quickly noticed that this particular building was undergoing renovations. Nick got out of the van and methodically started to unload the contents of our vehicle. I quickly followed suit and helped him to take my paintings inside the empty shop.

"What are we doing here, Nick?" I asked puzzled. How could anyone hope to do business selling paintings in a place this dusty with construction?

Nicholas told me to be quiet, say nothing and go finish setting things up inside the impromptu gallery. Meanwhile, he found a broom and tidied up. Satisfied with this quick manicure, Nick grabbed some signs from the van and set them out on the sidewalk. A couple of the signs had bright red arrows painted on them and the words 'OPEN NOW! GALLERY ENTRANCE' boldly advertising our location. In the store window, he placed another larger sign that loudly declared 'NEW GALLERY OPENING'. Almost immediately, people followed the arrows and streamed into the building. And to my amazement, they started buying. All I could think to myself was, "Wow! The owner must have been an angel to let us have this place." I was convinced that Nicholas was an absolute genius.

Suddenly, just as things were going so beautifully, a short, very angry looking man pushed his way through the happy crowd. Having jostled his way to the back of the store, he confronted Nicholas and me with a pointed finger that he shook with violence. The sweaty balding little man screamed out gruffly, "What's going on here? Where are my workers? Who do you think you are? This is my store!" The color of his face was scarlet red. I thought I saw smoke pouring from his ears. "Get out now!" the owner huffed. "Leave now or I am calling the cops!"

Before the hyperventilating store owner could say anything more, Nicholas calmly looked at the throng of art patrons and implored the sympathy of all by saying loudly, "I don't understand? We just paid the rent yesterday! Now he wants more money." Then Nick turned to the owner who was pulling out the last of the hairs on that shiny head and asked with a sly smile, "Why would you force us to go?"

The art loving public of this spontaneous gallery immediately pounced on the greedy little man with insults and scolding. How could he do this to a couple of poor starving artists? They shouted at him for being a heartless scrooge of a landlord. I could see we had an instant fan club! The enraged shop owner went berserk but managed to storm out of the building. He returned a few moments later with the police. These fine officers took a quick glance around assessing the situation and moved through the angry mob of fans requesting calm. Then one of the policemen saw Nick.

"Nicholas!" the officer said sternly. "How could you?" I looked at Nick with raised eyebrows but stayed mum. "I treat you well," continued the cop shaking his head. "Why do you do this to me? I want you out now!" he ordered.

"Of course, of course!" said Nicholas in cheerful compliance. He never liked trouble or bad feelings. "We were just about to close anyway. I apologize for the slight misunderstanding, Officer." Nick and the policeman were friends so we escaped the trespassing charge with only a warning and a stern reprimand.

We quickly packed the art display and the few remaining unsold paintings into the van and were soon on our way back to 53rd Street. I had not said a word throughout the entire course of events following Nick's instructions to be quiet. Now I needed to know what had happened there on Fifth Avenue at the so-called gallery of fine art.

"Oh," he answered chuckling. "You see, I know the area and that particular place quite well. The workers fixing the building leave for two hours to take their hour long lunch break. I move in for those two hours, sell paintings and, at the same time, mind the store while everyone is out. That way the workers have a long lunch and we have a gallery for two hours on the most expensive street in the world. You see how nicely it all works out."

I burst out laughing at this wonderfully logical arrangement. Looking at Nicholas I could see the twinkle of merriment in his sky-blue eyes. "Are you sure you're not really Irish?" I asked smiling.

New York City was a good teacher. I learned many things about work and struggle, adventure and delight that I had never imagined. I had the opportunity to meet many kinds of people from the rich and famous to the common man moving through the streets. I encountered the glamorous and beautiful, the kind and gentle as well as the ugly, the bizarre, and the evil. A cosmopolitan city like New York was truly a window with a view of humanity. I was drunk with success and felt the immortality of youth surging through me as I went about my escapades as an artist.

I had a display in front of a theater where I had the good fortune to meet many celebrities. One such person was the famous boxer, Mohammed Ali. He was playing himself in a show when, one day, to my surprise, he stopped and took the time to look at my work. He seemed to genuinely like the paintings. I watched as Mr. Ali passed by several times and he would warmly extend a greeting my way. One day he came over and closely inspected one of my newer paintings that had caught his fancy. Finally, after what seemed like hours, the boxer champ turned toward me and in a matter of fact tone addressed me, "My little Greek artist, how I like your style." I looked up at him with an air of true appreciation. Compared to me he was a really big man. "Please make some paintings for me someday. Won't you?" Mr. Ali continued.

"Sure. For you Mr. Ali-- anytime. It would be my pleasure!" I proudly responded. However, I never did hear from him again. Over the course of time, I was privileged to meet many other famous stars. Some of these icons of entertainment did buy my paintings, like Sammy Davis Jr. who liked my abstract art. Zsa Zsa Gabor purchased one as well. These were some of the golden moments of my life.

Nicholas and I were making a very good living, so when winter came and the New York City streets turn cold and icy, we flew like birds for warmer climates. Often we would travel to Greece for a couple of months to see family and friends. Eventually, we would migrate back to the States when our money was low and the warm spring weather had returned to New York. However, one particular winter we decided to do something different. A change was in order and we needed to do some exploring. Puerto Rico was rumored to be balmy and pleasant that time of year so Nicholas and I decided to see for ourselves. We left for the islands. It was a fabulously lazy time for us, swimming in the turquoise sea, playing a hot game of volleyball on the white sandy beach, relaxing in a hotel-casino, or sipping tropical drinks by the pool while watching spectacular sunsets. Winter was far away from our beach haven and from our sun soaked minds. Alas, our money was quickly disappearing. Fun can be expensive. We knew that it would soon be time to leave this tropical paradise and return to the concrete surroundings of New York City.

As fortune would have it, I was passing through the casino when I accidently ran into a distinguished looking gentleman playing at one of the tables. I excused myself and made my introductions. He was a professor of art from the University of Puerto Rico. "This is a wonderful accident," I thought to myself. I then regaled him with my knowledge of painting and explained that I was an artist inspired and trained in Europe. He seemed genuinely impressed and we arranged a meeting in the hotel lobby where I would show him some of my work. It was a fortunate thing that as a traveling plein-air artist my work could go wherever I went. He was waiting when I arrived and I gladly unveiled my paintings for him. He stood there for a few serious moments.

"These are wonderful. You have such raw talent," he exclaimed in accented English. "I have a proposal for you Señor Artist. Would you care to honor my class by spending a day with them? I am sure they will benefit well from your instruction."

I was surprised by his offer. Of course, I agreed. The next day I was a guest professor in a legitimate school of fine art. The professor compensated me well. Now, Nicholas and I could fly home to New York City.

"Tropically Pink" by George and Melanie Petridis

"Caribbean Cove"

This painting was inspired from a vacation to the beautiful hot and sultry island of Puerto Rico. Nicholas and I flew like birds to this wonderfully warm retreat in order to escape New York City's icy winter grasp.

It was the middle of April. Spring had finally come to New York City. The weather was cool and pleasant, ideal for displaying my paintings on the street. With just ten dollars in my pocket, I was beginning to worry whether I would have enough money to get through the week? Nicholas and I had spent all our cash in Puerto Rico. But this was New York, a place where miracles happened every day.

As I was contemplating my current financial situation, a black stretch limousine eased to a stop in front of my display. The chauffeur came around the car and opened the rear door. With an air of familiarity, an expensively dressed middle-aged man exited his luxurious automobile and approached me with a hand extended in greeting.

"Hi! George! How are you? How was Puerto Rico?"

I stepped back feeling more than a little surprised. I had never seen this man before. "Who are you? How do you know me? How did you know I was in Puerto Rico?" I fired questions at this stranger standing before me.

He apologized for alarming me and introduced himself as Mr. Leonard. "Please just call me Lenny," he said. He then continued with an explanation of how he and his wife went to a gallery on 86th Street a few weeks ago. His wife, Barbara, wanted to buy some of my paintings and also meet the artist. The gallery owner told them that I was on vacation in Puerto Rico and would be here on the fourteenth of April. "Now please, if you would pick up your paintings and come with me. My wife is dying to meet you!" Lenny smiled and waited for my response.

"Thank you Lord," I privately prayed. With help from the chauffeur, I quickly loaded my paintings into the van. Mr. Lenny had me follow his limo to 76th Street in

Manhattan, an area of expensive real estate without much commercial traffic. Things were looking up. We stopped in front of an elegant high-rise and Mr. Leonard said he lived on the top floor. Now, we were really looking up. Again, with help from the chauffeur, we carried the paintings up to the penthouse.

"Central Park"

Having made the skyward journey, we were rewarded with a greeting from the exuberant lady of the house. Barbara could hardly contain her excitement at the thought of having a favored artist in her home. "Welcome! Welcome!"She bade us come in and graciously directed the chauffeur and me to place the paintings in the living room. I arranged the pieces carefully around the room so they could be seen easily. "Very nice," she exclaimed. "I am Barbara." And then she kissed me lightly on both cheeks. "I am so very delighted to finally make your acquaintance, George! You are my favorite living artist."

I didn't know exactly how to take all of this. I had never known a new acquaintance to treat me as though we had been best friends for a long time. These people were complete strangers and yet so disarmingly like family.

Barbara grabbed my arm and pulled me into the next room where she proudly showed me the two paintings she had purchased from the gallery. "I am so proud of these. They are simply fabulous. I knew when I saw them that I had to meet you. It is so good of you to come here and bring me new beauties to admire. Shall we go see them now?"

We returned to the living room where Barbara went around to each painting and spent a moment of thoughtful repose. After careful consideration she turned to me, her face beaming in utter delight. "They are all so beautiful. It is difficult to choose which ones I like best." She looked at the art once more. Finally after a long pause she came to a decision. "I will take these," Barbara declared pointing at the paintings she wanted. Barbara pulled her husband aside. They talked for awhile and then Barbara came over to me intent on presenting me with something. "I hope this will do?" And she handed me seven thousand dollars. "If this isn't enough and you need more, please say so."

I was stunned as no one had ever offered that much money for my art. "No, no! This is more than enough," I told this lovely lady in appreciation. This money was more than sufficient to buy some frames for her since my new paintings had none. The rest of the money could go for a trip to Greece. At least that was my initial thinking. However, Barbara had plans too.

"George, my dear, I would like to host a party in your honor. I have many friends of means that would love to meet you," she announced to me. "You could demonstrate as well."

My eyes opened wide. I had to think about this most generous offer for a moment. "But I don't have enough paintings," I told her. "I will need some time to prepare."

"Is twenty days enough time for you?" Barbara

asked me. "If you require anything just feel free to ask. I will be more than glad to help." What a woman!

So I put my holiday plans on hold and went to work creating as many paintings as possible in the allotted twenty days. Before I knew it, the day of the party had arrived. The frames I had ordered for the paintings from the gallery on 86th Street were ready at the very last moment, so I hurried to pick them up. Because I couldn't find parking in front of the gallery I had to park on a side street instead. I left my van on 85th and walked to the gallery from there. It took about thirty minutes but, finally, I had the frames in hand and was anxious to go the party and what I thought would be a great success. As I rounded the corner I noticed something amiss about the van. As I got closer I could see that the van was missing things. In my shock and surprise, I almost dropped the frames. The wheels were gone. The vehicle was sitting on blocks and the doors were ajar. I hurried to see what else was gone. To my horror, the paintings and everything else including my art supplies had been stolen. The perpetrators, along with all my stuff, had quickly disappeared   into the streets and the shadows of buildings. I couldn't imagine anything worse happening. What could anyone possibly want with my easel and paints? Tears welled up in my eyes. I went back to the gallery and called the police and then I called Barbara. Half crying, I told her what had happened and that I could not, in my right mind, come to the party now.

Always the optimist, Barbara tried to calmly reassure me. "Oh, no my poor dear George, everyone is waiting for you here."

"But I don't even have my art equipment. They took everything I had."

"Listen to me George. I'm truly sorry about what happened but you must come. Surely you know someone from whom you can buy or borrow what you need. Please don't worry. Everything will be fine," Barbara reassured me. "I will send my car to pick you up."

The police soon came and my poor stripped vehicle was hauled away to the garage. Not long after a limousine pulled up in front of the gallery. I had to procure some necessary equipment before attending the party so I instructed the limo driver to take me to 53rd street. An artist friend of mine had a small display nearby. I went to see him and offered to rent his easel and paints for the evening and to buy his empty canvases. He was very happy to help. Finally, I felt relaxed enough to attend the party. As we pulled up to Lenny and Barbara's place I noticed at least twelve other limousines parked outside the penthouse. I hoped I wouldn't disappoint this elite gathering.

Barbara was waiting at the door for me appearing bubbly and cheerful. "George my dear, I'm so glad you made it! Everyone is waiting for you. You're our star for the evening." With that she ordered the chauffeur to help bring up the art equipment and frames.

I was feeling somewhat nervous and naked without my new paintings. Barbara took quick notice of this and calmed my fears. "George quit worrying. I took care of everything."She took me aside and slipped fourteen thousand dollars into my hand. I was puzzled. "George, I sold all of my paintings to everyone here," she explained. "Now you must paint me some new ones! So go get this party going!"

"New York, New York"

The party was lavish and lively. I started to relax and enjoy the music and hors d'oeuvres. This was penthouse Manhattan at its finest. Inspired by the evening, I had a new idea for a painting, 'Manhattan at Night'. The party goers gathered behind me as I created a new "masterpiece" before their eyes. One woman pushed a little closer to me than the other observers. "Mister Artist," she said to get my attention. "How much for this painting when it's finished? I really love where this is going!"

I was about to tell her the painting would cost five hundred dollars. To me that seemed like a high price. I wondered if I should ask for less? Ouch! Barbara purposely stepped on my foot and put her finger to her lips. She had gotten my attention. Before I could say anything, Barbara interrupted my conversation with my newest fan. "George meant to say the painting is two thousand five hundred dollars, my dear." Barbara then proceeded to give me a very valuable lesson in art economics. "Never undersell your work my dear George. People love your art and they will pay for it."

A favorite gathering place for some of us artists to hang out together was a restaurant called The Paramount, on 46th Street near Broadway. It was owned by a Greek and his Brazilian wife, Frankie and Eva. Over time we got to know each other well and became fast friends. Frankie

bought a number of paintings from me. Some of these he

proudly displayed in his restaurant. One evening, Nick and

I decided to have dinner there and celebrate my success at

Barbara's party. Now that we had some money, the two of

us could make plans for our winter migration. After a long

discussion Nick and I came up with a plan. Florida, the

'Sunshine State', would be the destination of this year's

migration. We had never been there. Besides, it was well

known that other artists would go to Florida for the winter

and would do rather well selling their art to 'snowbirds'

and tourists. I also had four cousins living there. This trip

would give me the chance to see them. Their mother, my

Aunt Sophia, had married a Greek American and moved to

New Castle, Pennsylvania many years ago. I was eager to

have a working vacation and meet the American half of my

family.

Chapter Five – Hurricane

Nick and I arrived to balmy weather and beautiful sunshine. The travel ads for Florida did not lie. We were warm with the knowledge that snowflakes could not touch us here. My cousins lived on the west coast of Florida and Nick and I ended up in the fishing village of Tarpon Springs. Tarpon Springs is a small iconic Greek community nestled in a quiet cove off the Gulf of Mexico. Many of its local inhabitants came from the island of Kalymnos in Greece. Fishing and sponge diving had always been the primary occupations of these people. The town hosted a number of Greek restaurants, shops, a nightclub, and the famous sponge docks where you could witness a live demonstration of helmeted divers gathering their prized catches off the sea floor. It was here that Nick and I met Bill, my first cousin. Bill, who had an uncanny resemblance to my brother, owned a local tavern, a marina, and a few shrimp boats in nearby New Port Richey. The youngest of my four cousins was all too happy to give us the grand tour. He introduced me to the American branch of my family.

One very sunny and humid morning, Bill offered to take us out on his new sailboat, the Black Jack. Bill had proudly won this most impressive vessel in a well-played game of cards. It was a good day to go out fishing and Bill was eager to test his ship's seaworthiness. With great enthusiasm, we joined him as shipmates for the virgin voyage of the Black Jack. Captain Bill was an experienced shrimper so Nick and I could rest assured that we were in excellent hands. He smoothly sailed the ship three miles out to the artificial reef where fishing was known to be great. The water glimmered in the morning sun like millions of diamonds as the spray splashed our faces. Wild dolphins played surfing games riding the bow of our magnificent boat. Wow! What a perfect day! We approached the reef and found a place to drop the anchor and begin fishing. As the noon hour neared the color of the sea began to change from green and turquoise to shades of gray. The wind started to pick-up and the water becomes choppy and frothy. The boat was rocking more and more with each slap of the waves. Huge ominous dark clouds towered high into the sky turning day into night. Bill reassured us that there was nothing to worry about but he quickly turned the Black

Jack around and headed back to port. Things went from bad to worse. We were worried. Claps of thunder boomed across the open sea while flashes of lightening opened the sky in a brilliant display of Nature's might. The wind sounded like a million screaming banshees. As the waves crested ever higher, they began crashing over the bow and the stern and steadily flooding our vessel. The little sailboat flipped and spun like a bathtub toy. Captain Bill desperately tried to guide the flailing ship through the churning angry black sea. Nick and I crossed ourselves and started praying. Mountains of water poured into our boat. Terrified, we shouted at Bill "we're sinking!"

"Bail!" shouted Bill. "Bail! Take a bucket and bail!" It was difficult to hear him above the howling gale. Bill tried calling for help on the radio. "Mayday! Mayday!" The call for help was never heard because the equipment was broken. "What a piece of junk!" screamed our captain in a fit of desperate anger.

Our frantic efforts at bailing weren't working either. The sea was pouring water into the ship's hull faster than we could pour it out. Bill tried to lower the anchor hoping it would keep us steady but the rope snapped. All was lost. The Black Jack was doomed to meet her fate at the bottom of the sea. Bill had previously mentioned that there were big sharks in the water and, now, we would provide a good meal. For the first time in my life, I truly believed I was going to die. How strange that the sea, my old friend, would take my body like my father's before me? I was not prepared to die. "God help me please!" I pleaded with the Divine. "What am I to do?" Then I heard all around me what sounded like whispered voices telling me to move my hands. It occurred to me to take off my white shirt and wave it in the air like a flag. I started to wave my shirt and scream for help above the roaring din of the storm.

Soon, I thought I saw an apparition, a faint silhouette visible beyond driving rain and between towering waves. But Nicholas and Bill saw it too. We all three could see another vessel coming our way. It was a large fishing boat. The fishermen started calling to us. We had been spotted and they were coming to our rescue! The crew approached as closely as they dared.

The Black Jack was listing badly and the wild sea made it too dangerous for the fishing boat to come directly alongside. One of the crew from the other craft called to us and threw lifesavers into the water. We jumped into the turbulent ocean, desperately grabbing for the buoys. My memory of the next few moments is a blur. Somehow, we were reeled aboard the fishing vessel. No sooner were we safely aboard, then we turned to see Cousin Bill's winning hand, the Black Jack, quickly disappear beneath the waves. The Black Jack would find rest at the bottom of the Gulf, becoming part of the reef and home to the creatures of the deep.

The fishermen watched our ship sink. "Do you know how lucky you guys are that we spotted your boat?" one of the crew asked us. "I barely saw, from the corner of my eye, that waving white flag of yours. It was obviously God's will that we rescue you!" The rain soaked fisherman kissed the medallion hanging from his necklace. "Thank you St. Andrew."

As we pulled into port, I could see that a crowd of people had gathered on the dock despite the foul weather. My cousins and their friends had come hoping to find us safely ashore. They had heard the storm warnings and were worried for our lives. Our rescue from the sudden squall and the doomed Black Jack seemed more miracle than accident. Had God whispered to me for his own purposes? A humbled artist, I painted a ship in an angry sea with a black sky parting to portray the end of a storm and the

Light that saves us all.

"Destiny's Storm"

The miraculous rescue that saved our lives from a sinking
sailboat in the middle of a raging storm on the Gulf of
Mexico was the inspiration for this painting. It was a
harrowing experience that brought me closer to God and
helped me to respect the awesome power of Nature.

Chapter Six – My Butterfly

Spring had again returned to the North and snowflakes were replaced by flower petals. The streets of New York City beckoned. I had a new painting, "After the Storm", to display for my always hungry art patrons. As I told the dramatic story of my harrowing adventure at sea and the miracle of being saved from a pitiless drowning, people would gather round me in large groups. They watched in amazement as the tale of the sea played itself out on my canvas. The painting brought the story to life. Several times I noticed a beautiful young woman in a light blue overcoat who would linger awhile after the crowd had dispersed. One day she stayed even longer, looking dreamily at one of my paintings. I approached her and asked if I could help with something. The girl was petite, slender, and elegantly graceful with hair like sunlit ripened wheat. She reminded me of a delicate butterfly. The young lady introduced herself as Julia.

"I'd like to buy this one," Julia said in a soft voice. She pointed to a floral painting that was perfect for a butterfly like herself. "This is so lovely. The colors are exquisite!"

Julia's voice had a slight lilt to it, different from the speech of New Yorkers. "Where are you from?" I asked, curious to know the origin of that softly accented voice. "Are you from the South?"

"How could you tell?" she responded with a slight smile showing on her lips. Her bright blue eyes sparkled with an inner light. This girl intrigued me.

Julia surprised me by asking if I would like to have lunch with her. Without a second thought, I quickly agreed. We found a small bistro and sat down to share a light meal and some conversation. She was a twenty-one year old ballerina. "You see, I am an artist too!" she proudly proclaimed. Julia was with a ballet company that performed at various theaters on Broadway. She was also taking dance lessons. Currently, her company was playing at New York City's entertainment landmark, Radio City Music Hall. "Would you like to come and see the show?" she asked hopefully.

"Oh yes!" I excitedly answered Julia without even thinking. "That would be great. Sure, I would love to come" Things were moving along rather quickly. I thought I would expand my artistic experience by visiting other mediums of creative expression.

Soon, we started seeing each other on a regular basis. I loved being in her presence. She was, for me, a magical experience.

One enchanted day, beautiful Julia and I decided to explore some of New York City's famous art attractions. Since we were on the Upper East Side of Manhattan, the Guggenheim Museum would be our first stop where we would look for new and breath-taking artistic treasures. Hand-in-hand, we toured the halls of the museum which was itself an architectural masterpiece. The paintings and sculptures were dazzling works of art by famous modern artists. Some were beautiful, some thought provoking and interesting, and some of the art was just plain weird. As we viewed piece after piece, we came upon one abstract painting that was very familiar to me. I stopped and stared long and hard at this picture. I could hardly believe my eyes. This painting was mine! How did one of my original artworks come to be exhibited in a famous place like the Guggenheim?

Julia pulled on my sleeve and pointed at something on the painting. I looked to see what had drawn her attention. It was the signature and it did not say 'George'. What? How could this be? Another name was showcased where mine was supposed to be. I was angry and confused. This was not right! I grabbed Julia's hand and together we went to find the curator for the exhibit.

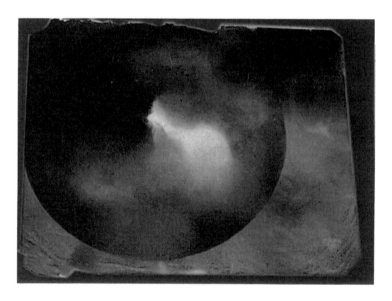

"The Space and the Earth"

Eventually, I was able to find him and explain my concerns. "This painting is mine!" I told him in an irritated voice. "I am the artist of 'The Spiral' and not that other name on my work!" As proof of my authorship of the piece, I showed him a photo of the painting I carried in my wallet. I was proud of this painting as it took me much time and effort to create. I continued by telling the curator how a dealer had come to my display and, after lots of haggling, had bought the painting. With some reluctance, the curator gave me the name of the man who had sold the painting to the museum. It was the same man! The manager also gave us the address where this unscrupulous seller could be found.

"Before the Guggenheim can allow you to change the name on this painting, you must find that dealer and have him give us written notice that the name on the painting is falsified and that you are, in fact, the artist," instructed the curator. "Only then can we allow you to sign the artwork. That is the best I can do for you." He was firm about museum policy.

Now, I had to find a forger and force him to admit that he was a scoundrel. Julia and I went to find this con artist. But the address he gave the museum was false and his name was most likely an alias. Because I could not obtain the declaration of falsehood, the Guggenheim would not allow me to sign my own painting. I was deeply offended by this crime and the unending injustice that followed. Millions of people have seen and will see my painting but I will never become known for my creation. I now know the pain of having been robbed of what is a part of me. Art is an extension of the artist's unique inner person. It is a culmination of memories and emotions, and a personal vision of how the world appears interpreted through the artist's singular prism. This is a type of theft that leaves long lingering feelings of bereavement. Welcome to the darker aspects of the rarefied world of art.

Julia and I were good together and I eventually proposed marriage. Although she could be emotionally distant at times, I had faith in our future. She danced and I painted. It was a beautiful match. One day Julia received a telephone call from her family in New Orleans. The news was bad. Julia quickly descended into sadness mixed with anxiety. Her mother was very ill and she needed her daughter to come home as soon as possible. When Julia hurriedly departed for New Orleans, I reluctantly stayed behind to attend to business and, hopefully, complete the arrangements for our wedding. I missed her.

Meanwhile, an event came up which allowed me to try something new. Good old Nicholas who had that nose for opportunity learned of a show in the Staten Island Mall for travelling artists. This was the first time I had heard the term 'travelling artists'. What artist didn't travel? The concept of a shopping mall was also new to me. At least fifty artists from around the country would be in attendance and there was still room for more. So I applied and was accepted into the show. I was excited by this new gig and it would be a pleasant distraction from missing Julia. Happily, I set up my display and waited to see what would happen. Thursday, the first day of the show, was a miserable rainy day. Still, people came to shop and I didn't have to worry about getting wet. There were many artists competing for patrons but, usually, the art patron makes choices based on personal taste rather than price.

As I demonstrated my technique, a crowd would often gather to watch me paint. People like to see something new being created. Some of these onlookers would engage in conversation with me inquiring about the stories behind the paintings and the life experiences of the artist. Often, such conversation would lead to a purchase with the added benefit of new friendships being formed.

By early afternoon a group people were gathered at my display and were seriously looking at the artwork. I still had not sold a painting but this was the first day and there was plenty of time. As I cheerfully worked on a floral painting using my palette knife to sculpt out colorful flower petals, I saw a young, well-dressed man quickly approach my display. He took a rapid look around only scanning the paintings briefly and then hurriedly approached me. With suspicious alacrity he asked, "Are you the artist? How much do you want for this picture?" And he pointed at a large seascape. I paused and looked at him for a moment as I was surprised by his abrupt manner. I quoted him a price. He proceeded to point at five more large paintings. "I'll take these six. What will you take for the lot?" He immediately sat down at my table and pulled out a pen and check waiting for my reply. A hint of a smile belied his otherwise serious and businesslike face.

"Ah, the price for these six paintings is forty eight hundred dollars," I told him, while at the same time, I was convinced that there was something wrong with this picture. The fellow was much too detached and made no real inquiry or conversation about the art or the artist. In fact, he had never actually spent any time looking at the paintings. They were chosen with less care than you would use to pick apples at a grocer's stand. I silently examined him and could feel his aura. Just as he started to write the check, I stopped him. "Sir, I don't take checks, only cash." I told him. "I can't accept that."

The man's face flushed with anger. "What do you mean? My check isn't good enough for you? Do you expect me to carry around this amount of money? You are really crazy!" he blurted out. Was he truly offended by my refusal to accept his check for payment?"

I thought to myself that perhaps I was making a very expensive mistake. After all, this was four thousand eight hundred dollars that I was about to lose. But I stood by my first instinct. Something was bothering me. "No sir, I cannot accept this check!" I stated firmly. After that final proclamation, the man stormed off into the crowded mall. I hoped I hadn't guessed wrong.

The next day, I saw the police speaking with various artists in the mall. They came to my booth as well. The cops started questioning me about the man who tried to purchase my art the day before. I told them how he tried to buy six of my best paintings but the sale failed when I refused to take his check.

"Good thing!" one of the policemen exclaimed. "This man is a check forger." The officer went on to say that the thief had written bad checks and made off with a number of artworks from paintings to metal sculpture. The other artists had discovered that those generous checks were no good when they tried to cash them. Thank goodness I had listened to that little voice in my head that gave me a bad feeling about the man and his purchases. I felt sorry for my fellow artists who had been duped and robbed of their work. I wondered why his abrupt manner and coolness did not alert the others.

The show did turn out to be a success. As always, I sold my paintings to honest people and true art loving patrons. As a bonus, I also found a new and exciting way to display my paintings to a much larger and more diverse audience.

I returned to Manhattan a happy man and couldn't wait to call Julia and tell her the good news.

Not long after the Staten Island Mall show, I received a call from my old friends, Lenny and Barbara. They had exciting news to share and wanted to meet with me to discuss a business proposal. I suggested we go to my

friend's restaurant, the Paramount. Frankie, the owner,

greeted us and showed us to our table.

"I see we all love the same art and artist," remarked

Barbara laughing as she gazed at my paintings which were

gracing the walls of the restaurant. "It is because of this,"

she continued, "that Lenny and I have a very important and

exciting offer to make to you."

"You see, Barbara and I would like to open a

gallery for you on Madison Avenue," said Lenny excitedly.

He was a very successful businessman and would not

suggest this venture if he thought it would fail. And of

course he had planned out every detail. So we sat and

conversed about the proposed gallery, a fifty-fifty

arrangement for the parties concerned. This was a dream

come true- to have my own gallery. It would take about a

week to draw up the contracts. And so it was agreed. I could not wait to surprise Julia with the good news.

A lot can happen in one week and unfortunately, it was happening to me. A phone call from New Orleans changed my plans forever. It was Julia. She sounded very different from the girl I had known in New York. Her voice was strange and I knew something was terribly wrong. She pleaded with me to come to New Orleans as quickly as possible but she would not tell me why. Was she hurt? Was she sick? How about her Mother? Julia did not explain. She was mumbling incoherently between heaving sobs. Then, suddenly and without warning, she hung up. I was desperate and determined to find her. I left in a rush for New Orleans. I put off signing the papers that would have given me a gallery in a very prestigious place and the potential for limitless success with my art career in order to save my precious butterfly.

In a state of panic I arrived in the middle of a sticky hot Louisiana day. There was a brief downpour and then the burning sun came out turning what should have been a refreshing shower into a warm steam bath. I went to search for my dear Julia. What I found both shocked and angered me. She was living in her mother's tiny house without her mother. The house was on a street not far from the French Quarter located in an inner-city area rife with low life criminal activity. And to my great consternation I could see that a lot of strange men were coming and going from her house. My greatest anguish, however, came from seeing my bride-to-be. The beautiful ballerina butterfly had morphed into a sickly, pale, zombie like creature. I found a place to stay and begged Julia to come and stay with me. But even after she was living with me, Julia would invent alibis and sneak back to her mother's place. Her mother was still hospitalized. I soon discovered that Julia was hooked on heroin and keeping company with pushers and

Johns. She wanted money from me to feed this filthy habit.

I was angry and dismayed. How was I to rescue this once

vibrant fellow artist from destroying herself? I felt utterly

betrayed. She had hidden this ugly secret from me for a

very long time. Her sometimes distant behavior and erratic

moods were not those of an eccentric artist but of a junky.

Julia's return to her old neighborhood in New Orleans only

made the problem worse as she reconnected with old

acquaintances. One morning, after she had snuck out of my

place, I went to her mother's house to find her. No one was

there. I saw some neighbors and asked if they had seen

Julia. They told me that earlier in the morning the sounds

and lights of ambulances and police cars had jarred them

from their sleep. Someone who looked like Julia had been

taken from the house on a stretcher and transported to the

hospital. The rumor was a drug overdose. I hurried to the

nearest medical center but arrived too late. The butterfly

was gone. My world had been flipped upside-down. Grief

was now my only companion, feeding on a deep love for a creature I could not help. In order to find solace I needed to go home. And home for me was Greece. So with the little money I had left, I bought a plane ticket and left my new world fantasy behind, returning to Hellas, my birthplace.

"Home"

"Flowers for my Butterfly"

Chapter Seven – Destiny's Dream

My mother welcomed me with a mother's arms. But, even with her love and support, I could not find comfort. I was spiraling downward to the depths of emotional despair from which some men find no escape. I didn't know if I could climb my way out of that dark, suffocating place. Six forever months had come and gone. My depression was deepening, etching marked changes on my appearance and demeanor. A scraggly beard had sprouted to cover my sunken face. My hair was unkempt and I was gaunt and steadily losing weight. My eyes appeared dull and hollow like a statue's as I stared at the mirror. The world had betrayed me.

"Moonlight Surf"

Every day, I would go to the beach alone and wander around. Life was so empty that even beauty was elusive. I could not paint. What had happened to destiny? I didn't really care. Depression's pain is not reserved for the afflicted person. It has a way of hurting others. My dear mother, who had suffered so much in her own life, was now anguished because of me. She tried her best to console me and offered her caring words and deeds in my time of need. But she was becoming discouraged because I remained drowsy with grief despite her best efforts to revive me.

One restless night of intermittent sleep, a dream of sorts came to me. The vision revealed a place of peace, a 'Stairway to Heaven'. I could not shake the image from my mind. It was like God was trying to show me the way up and away from this self-loathing. Slowly, it dawned on me that my poor mother did not deserve this grief, not from her son. I started to feel sorry for someone other than George.

It was an unusually beautiful night as I walked the beach alone. It was the first time since returning home to Greece that I actually saw the stars twinkling in the deep dark of the sky above and heard the waves gently caressing the shore. A lone gull who seemed to be there waiting for me was my sole companion. I saw that the moon was full as its radiance reflected on the water, reminding me of my childhood. The further I walked the more the happy memories of my youth came flooding back. I could swear I heard sweet, romantic music drifting across the calm of the sea coming from the ghost of Trocadero. As these pleasant memories played over and over in my mind, the storm that had engulfed my soul began to dissipate. Finally, a small voice like a gentle sea breeze came to me. It was very clear. "George, you don't have to do this anymore. Go home." The urge to run back to the house abruptly shortened my evening reminiscences.

Standing in front of my house I waited for something. And then it came. I was suddenly overcome with a torrential rush of emotion. I prayed in desperation, "Lord, I don't want to be a dead soul anymore. Please help me." God answers in his own way. I was instantly filled with an overwhelming urge to do something I hadn't thought of in months. I needed to paint!

My mother was waiting up for me when I entered the house, as she did every night. "Are you hungry?" She pressed me to eat something but I gently refused.

"Mother, please, not right now. I need to do something," I told her tenderly. "Please understand." With that I went to my room and shut the door. As I opened the heavy sliding panels that led to the veranda, the bedroom flooded with an ethereal white light from the moon. It was like Heaven had opened its windows. Trancelike, I took an empty canvas that had been gathering dust and propped it up on a table. I then took out my neglected paints, squeezing the colors out onto a makeshift palette. Finally, after months of sloth and misery, I began painting again. Hours passed and the cool whiteness of the moonlit night gave way to the golden light of dawn and a new day. I painted hypnotically without stopping to eat or rest. Startled from my quiet ecstasy by a soft knock on the bedroom door, I stopped painting. My mother's sweet, worried voice was asking permission to come inside.

"Son, I have brought you some coffee and koulourakia. Are you alright?" she tempted me from outside the closed door with morning refreshment.

Exhausted from my nocturnal marathon, I slowly opened the door to let her into the room. My mother peered through the open doorway and then tentatively stepped through. Her dark brown eyes grew very big and her mouth opened letting out a tiny but audible gasp. She almost dropped the tray of Greek coffee and breakfast cookies. She quickly set the tray down on a nearby nightstand and put her now open hands to her face. My mother closely approached the painting and stood before it for a few moments without saying a word, transfixed by the sight before her. She turned toward me and took my hand in hers. Tears welled up in her eyes.

"George, did you do this?" asked my mother. It was not really a question but more like an affirmation.

"Yes Mother," I answered. "With God's help I did this."

"Oh my dear boy, I have been praying for this!" She embraced me and kissed my cheek. "This painting is so beautiful, so beautiful. I have never seen you paint, George. This is truly a blessed miracle from God!"

I embraced my mom with a long and grateful hug. "Mother, I dedicate this painting to you," I whispered softly in her ear. Now, we both had tears in our eyes. "You have given me everything," I continued. My voice was raspy with emotion and weariness. "Mom, I love you with all my heart and so I am giving you this painting. God came to me last night and showed me a dream. It was a place where you have been, Mama. I saw this beautiful lake and a waterfall coming down from the mountain. There were animals with you and a bright light from Heaven. You see, this painting was truly meant for you."

My mother squeezed my hand tightly. "I prayed for you so many times, my dear George," she cried. "Son, this is God's gift to you. All talent comes from Him. You must use it for good. And no matter what happens, never forget that." She forced a slight smile and together we stood there in that light filled room. I believe in miracles. I have seen them happen and they are as real as tragedy. That night, a miracle guided me back to my life's path, my destiny.

A noise outside startled us from the sublime back to the present. The sound came from the gate at the entrance to our yard. We both looked at each other. The moment we shared together was broken by a voice seemingly familiar but unexpected calling "George! George! Are you there?" My mother released my hand and went to see who this visitor was who called for her son.

Elpiniki greeted the man who introduced himself to her. He asked once more for me and so she opened the gate and let him inside.

"George is in there," she said pointing to my room. Following her direction, the man came to stand at the threshold of my wondrous nighttime art studio, formerly my bedroom.

I didn't see my visitor at first as my back was turned. I was lost in thought while adding a few final touches to the painting. Then, with great surprise, I heard a deep voice that was not my mother's.

"George! Did you do this?" asked the voice. I swung around quickly, not believing my ears. "Oh my word, it's you!" I exclaimed, completely shocked. My eyes confirmed what my ears had heard. "Frankie, what are you doing here?" It was my friend from New York City. He was the owner of the Paramount restaurant and a collector of my art. "How did he ever find me?" I wondered.

Frankie told me how he and others had come to know of the tragic events of New Orleans and that, afterwards, I had gone to Greece. "George, you have been gone so long. With no word from you everyone has started to worry. So many people are asking for you. They are waiting for you to come back to New York. We miss you."

I looked at him feeling somewhat disoriented. I am really missed? In my struggle with depression, I had forgotten about everyone and everything. Frankie's admonitions that people missed me and worried about me seemed like revelations.

"George, my friend, tell me about this painting. You know I must have it." Frankie had changed the subject back to art. "This painting is outstanding." And he stood there in front of my newest creation awaiting my response.

I looked at my friend who had traveled thousands of miles to see me and I shook my head. "No Frankie! I did this for my mother," I replied back to him. "Anyway, it is still unfinished."

My mother, who had overheard the conversation, came quietly into the room. I had turned to continue working on the painting. She used the opportunity to grab Frankie by the arm and quickly pull him outside the doorway. "I want to get to know you better," she said to Frankie. "After all, I do not know too many of my son's friends from America."

After they had disappeared outside of earshot, my mother turned to Frankie and took his hands into hers. "You are the miracle I have been praying for. George has been alone and not himself for a very long time. I want you to have this painting. It will help him to get back on his feet." Mothers have an innate wisdom and selflessness about them that no son can truly explain. She knew that Frankie buying my first post-depression painting would allow me to pick up my brush, fly back to New York and be productive again. The two ever so quietly came to an arrangement and then stepped back into the bedroom.

"George, your friend is going to buy this," my mother stated emphatically. "It is alright by me. I want you to buy a ticket and go back to New York."

Frankie broke into the conversation. "George, when you have returned to the States and started working again, you can buy this painting back for your mom."

"Frankie and I agree," said my mother. "Please do this for me. Save yourself George. We love you."

An airline ticket lifted me across the ocean and I found myself once more in the land of dreams and possibilities as an artist reborn. Life had closed one chapter and opened another, leaving me to wonder what the Good Lord had in store. Whenever my body or soul was in danger, He had always spared me. He gave me a divine gift as well. I will share this gift with an overwhelming sense of gratitude. I will paint as long as the Good Lord allows. Art is not a profession from which I can retire. It is my mission, my calling and my destiny to help others see the beauty that is all around us. Beauty can delight us, sustain us and, somehow, redeem us. I do not care to be a senator or a judge or a ruler of nations. I wish only to walk this earthly path as an artist of the people.

"Stairway to Heaven"

One dark night of my life, God came to me with a beautiful dream. This wonderful vision saved me and helped me to find my way back onto the path of light and beauty.

Epilogue – The Case of Mary

Art has a universality about it. It doesn't obey time and, therefore, never grows old or useless. Instead, it stands up to the rigors of the ages and can be appreciated over and over by countless eyes and generations. The artist immortalizes him or herself through their work.

Here is Mary's story.

One day back in the early Seventies a young woman passed by my display on 53rd Street in New York. An abstract painting caught her admiring eye. She knew from that moment that she just had to have that art piece. Mary turned to me and asked for the price. I told her it was sixty dollars.

"That's all? Please don't sell this painting," she implored. "I am coming right back." And with that, she hurriedly left for a nearby bank to obtain the precious sixty dollars. As she promised, Mary quickly returned and paid for her first original artwork. The smile on her face was priceless. I carefully parceled the painting and told her how to hold it as part of the painting was still wet.

Mary had to take the train home to Brooklyn. It was a fretful trip because she was certain someone or something would touch her prized possession. To her surprise, the wet painting made the entire trip completely unscathed. Finally, it was safe at home. She took great care to unwrap her new abstract art piece and propped it up against some furniture. Mary stood there for a few moments admiring this thing of beauty that gave her so much joy. As she left the room to find a hammer and a nail on which to hang the painting, her rambunctious four year old son bounced into the living room. Temptation beckoned and a tiny finger met with the wet paint on the canvas.

Even with that small blemish, Mary continued to love and cherish what would be her first and only original painting. More than forty years later after much searching, she happily found my phone number and called just to say how much that painting has meant to her and to see if her one and only favorite artist was still alive and well. That call made my day. This is what art is all about.

True art is indeed timeless and priceless because it is the gift of beauty that people of every generation need in their lives. Those graced by God with the ability to create such splendor are obligated to share that splendor with others. I want the youth of the world to know this: Life is beautiful. Our children must be taught to walk the path of beauty and it is my hope that this book will open their hearts to that opportunity.

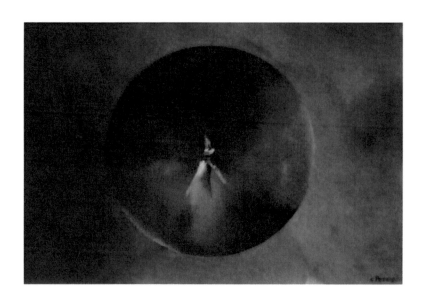

"Mary's Painting"

Synopsis

George Petridis was born and raised in Athens, Greece. He is well travelled and has a broad, cosmopolitan experience in life. This experience is seen in his art. He has been painting more than 50 years having discovered his talent when he was twenty years old. George studied under a well-known Dutch artist where he learned to employ his own unique and creative style of painting. An abstract and impressionistic artist of land, sea, and cityscapes, George has exhibited and sold his work internationally for many years. George's paintings of his beloved Greece, stormy seas, abstract florals, and Parisian street scenes are found in many private collections throughout the world. Patrons of his work hail from the United States, Greece, Australia, Canada and more. Now in his 70's, George continues to leave his artistic legacy for generations to come.

George at the mall

About the Author

Melanie Stephenson – Petridis was born and raised in Western Pennsylvania. She has pursued artistic expressions since early childhood. Her father, a talented artist, and her mother, a trained artist, encouraged Melanie's artistic endeavors by supplying her with their own art tools and paints. They also hosted parties that included other artist friends who in turn gave encouragement and valuable critiques. One of Melanie's biggest inspiration and muse for painting and drawing was the horse. The horse is therefore often featured somewhere in her art if not as the main subject. Melanie has received many awards and recognition for her art and illustrations. The goal of her art is to bring a subject to life and tell a story. Melanie paints in a realistic – semi-impressionistic style. She is basically self-taught but inspired by others. Her formal education includes environmental geography and anthropology. She is a Naturalist. This education has helped Melanie use her art as an ambassador to the natural world by engaging people in Nature's beauty be it animal, plant or scenery. Her paintings feature equestrian scenes, wildlife and outdoor Nature scenes, and historical and architectural subjects. Melanie's most unusual art includes a montage of Russian scenes from before 1917. Of course, the Russian troika horse team was the main inspiration with the unique architecture and romantic fairy tale landscape completing the picture. The Russian themed paintings make for great storytelling. She is also very well-known for all things equestrian from formal horse portraits to foxhunting and thoroughbred racing scenes. Wildlife scenes and honoring her Native American heritage is also prominent in her work. Her artist husband, George Petridis, encouraged her to do fine art as a profession. Today, Melanie's work is found in many international collections and she continues to produce new and interesting art pieces. Melanie is also becoming well-known for her Nature photography. She uses the idea of telling a story and the fundamentals of painting techniques to turn wildlife photos into art. She hopes to continue a tradition of creating valuable masterpieces with universal appeal for all generations to appreciate – and to open Human eyes to see God's Great Creation.

About the Co-Author

Nicholas Orfan is a practicing physician living in Maryland. Born in New York, he has studied and worked in various cities throughout the United States and Europe. He has written numerous scholarly articles for scientific journals. This is his first effort at a story for general interest readers.

"Poseidon's Gift" c1993 by Artists: Melanie and George

Petridis

This painting is a collaboration between two very different

artists who can come together in one moment of singular

beauty.